COOL 6 English

PUPIL'S BOOK

Günter Gerngross • Herbert Puchta

CAMBRIDGE

The Alphabet Rock

Welcome back now, everyone.
Learning can be lots of fun.
Enjoy your time in class again
With Emma and her clever friends.
Let's rock until the English lesson ends.

One, two, three – a, b, c,
Sing and dance and rock with me,
yeah.
D, e, f, g, h, i, j,
Come on, it's a lovely day.
K, l, m, join in again, hey, hey!

N, o, p, q, r, s, t,
Clap your hands and rock with me.
Sing u and v and w.
Touch your nose and shake your head,
Turn around, shout x and y and z.

2 Find the classroom objects.
Then spell the words.

[two]

2

1 School friends

2 **3** Listen and read. Then ask a classmate.

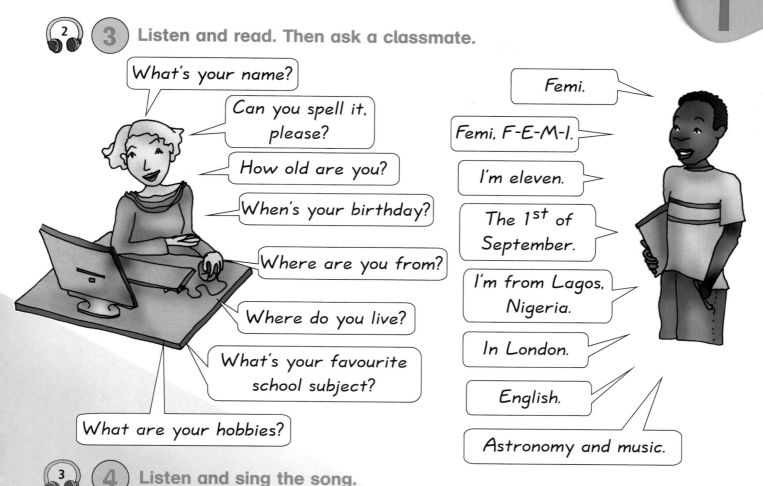

What's your name?

Can you spell it, please?

How old are you?

When's your birthday?

Where are you from?

Where do you live?

What's your favourite school subject?

What are your hobbies?

Femi.

Femi, F-E-M-I.

I'm eleven.

The 1st of September.

I'm from Lagos, Nigeria.

In London.

English.

Astronomy and music.

3 **4** Listen and sing the song.

Back to School

Today's my first day at school
And it's not cool, and it's not cool.
I'm not from here, I feel blue,
I don't know him, or her, or you!
New town, new school,
New faces, new places.
Who's she? Who's he?
I just don't know!
Do they like me?

Today's my first day at school

And it's not cool, and it's not cool.
I'm not from here, I feel blue,
I don't know him, or her, or you!
New town, new school,
New faces, new places.

Who's she? Who's he?
Do they want to be my friends?
I don't know!
Do they want to be my friends?
I just don't know!

School friends

 5 6 **Listen and point. Then ask a classmate about the school subjects.**

Science – Drama
Maths – History
Music – Geography
English – Spanish
Information Technology
PE (Physical Education)

Do you like Geography?

What's your favourite subject?

Yes, I do.

Music.

7 **Talk about yourself.**

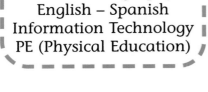

I get up at … .

In the afternoon I often…

My best friend's name is … .

He/She is … years old.

We sometimes…

I like…

My favourite hobby is … .

I want to be a … .

seven o'clock – half past seven
quarter to eight – quarter past eight

play with friends – play football – read – listen to music

11 – 12 – 13 – 14

ride our bikes – play table tennis – go swimming – go to the cinema

books – stamps – comics computers – CDs – my dog my cat

swimming – riding my bike collecting coins

a doctor – a pilot – a teacher a computer programmer a writer

8 Our world: **About me**
Read and do the quiz.

Samshaad

Lena

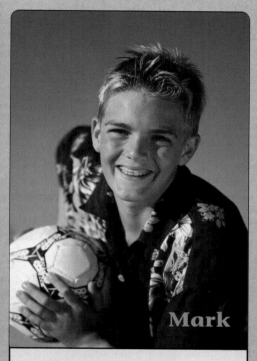

Mark

Hi, I'm Samshaad.
I live in India. I get up at six o'clock in the morning. Then I help my mother in the house. I walk to school.
There are fifty-two children in my class. We don't wear a school uniform. I love learning. I want to be a teacher.

My name is Lena. I'm from Nigeria in Africa. I'm eleven. I don't go to school everyday because I help my family. I get up at half past six and I start work at seven o'clock. I sell mangos and bananas in the street. I like talking to different people. I want to have my own little shop.

Hi, I'm Mark. I'm from Western Australia. I'm twelve and I live on a farm. The farm is 400 kilometres from a town, so I can't go to school. My lessons start at nine on TV. I e-mail my homework to my teacher. She sometimes comes to the farm to help me. I want to be a farmer.

Quiz. **How many questions can you answer?**

1. Are there fifty two children in Samshaad's class?
2. Do Samshaad's parents live in Africa?
3. Is Lena from Australia?
4. Do Mark's lessons start at eight on TV?
5. Is the farm 400 kilometers from a town?

1 School friends

6 9 Sounds like fun

> **K**ate is a **k**id that
> li**k**es **K**arate class,
> **k**arao**k**e and **k**ites.

10 Language puzzle

Do you like London?	Yes, I do.	No, I don't.
Are you from London?	Yes, I am.	No, I'm not.
Is London the capital of England?	Yes, it is.	No, it isn't.

11 Write about yourself.

My name is ... and I'm ...
years old.
I live in...   I like...
I don't like...
My favourite subject at school
is ... .
I want to be ... .

12 Project: **Make a poster about your best school friend.**

☻ MY BEST SCHOOL FRIEND ☻

This is our street and our city: Edinburgh, the capital of Scotland.

I'm Samantha Macadam. Here I'm with my best friend Sally. We go to school together. We live in the same street.

This is our ballet class. We love ballet. We want to be professional dancers.

2 Save the planet!

  1 Listen and sing the song.

Our Planet

It's a wonderful, beautiful world.
Let's work together to make it better,
With every boy and every girl
Finding solutions to stop pollution.
We need to save the planet, plant more trees,
Keep the rivers and oceans clean,
Protect the dolphins and the whales!
Stop wasting the resources and recycle them.

It's a wonderful, beautiful world.
Let's work together to make it better,
With every boy and every girl
Finding solutions to stop pollution.
We need to use less water, burn less oil,
Walk or ride our bikes,
Protect the fish and animals!
Stop wasting the resources and recycle them.

It's a wonderful, beautiful world.

picking up litter – planting a tree
helping animals – riding a bicycle
recycling – using less water

2 Ask a classmate.

What are you doing to save the planet?

I'm recycling my rubbish.

9 [nine]

7

8

9

10

11 12

Save the planet!

  4 Listen and point. Then ask a classmate.

> What's the tiger doing?

> It's hunting an animal.

tiger – dolphin – whale
monkey – eagle – turtle

hunting – jumping
swimming – flying
climbing – walking

5 Play the game. Describe and guess the animal.

It lives in India.
It eats other animals.
It's got black and yellow fur.
It's in danger of extinction.

It lives in China.
It only eats bamboo leaves.
It's got black and white fur.
It's in danger of extinction.

It lives on a farm.
It eats grass.
It's got long legs.
It's not in danger
of extinction.

panda bear – tiger
kingfisher – horse
rabbit – sheep

It lives in a hole.
It eats plants.
It's got long ears.
It's not in danger of
extinction.

It lives in a hole.
It eats fish.
It's got blue feathers.
It's a bird in danger of
extinction.

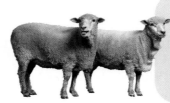

It lives on a farm.
It eats grass.
It's got white wool.
It's not in danger of
extinction.

Does it eat grass?

Does it live on a farm?

Is it small?

Has it got feathers?

Is it in danger of extinction

Is it a kingfisher?

No, it doesn't.

No, it doesn't.

Yes, it is.

Yes, it has.

Yes, it is.

Yes, it is.

Our world: Our environment
Read and do the quiz.

The black rhino

The black rhino lives in East Africa. It eats fruit and leaves. The black rhino is not black, it's grey. Why is it called black? Black rhinos love mud and they often take baths in mud. When they come out, they look black. People kill rhinos and sell their horns to make medicine. But it isn't real medicine because it doesn't cure. The black rhino is in danger of extinction.

The dolphin

Dolphins live in many different parts of the sea. They hunt small fish for food. The dolphin is in danger of extinction. Why is this? It's because pollution and over fishing are killing the dolphin's food. Fishing nets are also killing the dolphins. What can we do? Fishermen need to change the way they fish and we all need to think about water pollution.

The orangutan

Orangutans live in the tropical forests of Sumatra and Borneo. They eat fruit. There are not many orangutans in Sumatra and Borneo today. The orangutan is in danger of extinction. Why is this? It's because they only live in large tropical forests. People are burning the forests and cutting down the trees. When people cut down these forests the orangutans haven't got any place to live.

Quiz. How many questions can you answer?

1. Has the black rhino got a horn?
2. Does the black rhino live in East Africa?
3. Is the dolphin in danger of extinction?
4. Is over fishing helping the dolphin?
5. Does the orangutan eat fruit?
6. Has the orangutan got any place to live?

Yes, it is. / No, it isn't.
Yes, he does. / No, he doesn't.
Yes, it has. / No, it hasn't.

7 **Sounds like fun**

How does a loud cow sound? Do you know?
Yes! It sounds like the cold wind blowing in
the snow!

8 **Language puzzle**

Is it small?

Yes, it is.

Has it got feathers?

Yes, it has.

Does it eat grass?

No, it doesn't.

What's the tiger doing?

It's hunting.

9 **Write about an animal in danger of extinction.**

It lives in...
It eats/hunts...
It's got...
Why is it in danger
of extinction?
Because...
What can we do?
We can...

10 **Project:** **Make a poster about things we can do to save the planet and help other animals.**

3 Free time

  Listen and sing the song.

Free Time

I want to have some fun
But I don't know what to do.
I like to swim and run
And I like to play football too.
Where can I go? What can I do?
Where can I go? Can I play with you?

There are lots of things to do
And lots of friends to see.
You can go to the swimming pool
Or you can go to the cinema with me.
Come on, let's go! There's lots to see and do.
Come on, let's go! Our friends can all come too.

There are many different shops
For music, clothes and books.
A sports centre for sports
And a supermarket just for food.
You can ride your bike
Or you can walk around,
Or you can go by bus
When you go into town.

Thanks for telling me
The things that I can do.
And when my time is free
I want to have some fun with you.
To go into town, to shop or swim or play
Or spend the afternoon in an internet cafe.

2 **Ask a classmate.**

Where can we go?

We can go to the cinema.

swimming pool
sports centre – cinema
cycle path – internet cafe
supermarket – music shop
clothes shop – bookshop

15 [fifteen]

Free time

4 Listen and point.
Then talk to a classmate.

chocolate cake
crisps
hotdogs
milkshake
pizza
ice cream
cola
salads

Wow! I'm hungry. Are there any sandwiches?

Yes, there are.

Is there any orange juice?

No, there isn't any.

Are there any doughnuts?

Yes, there are some.

5 Ask a classmate.

Where can we go?

Let's go to the bookshop.

What can we do there?

We can buy some books.

BOOKS CLOTHES CD'S
MARKET
SHOPPING CENTRE

CHEMIST

CINEMA

SUPERMARKET

MUSIC SHOP

BOOKSHOP

CLOTHES SHOP

TAKEAWAY

SPORTS CENTRE

LIBRARY

BANK

INTERNET CAFE

Our world: Pastimes
Read and do the quiz.

I'm Raul from Rio de Janeiro. I spend a lot of my free time playing football near my house.
I want to be a professional footballer like Ronaldo.
I also like swimming. There isn't a swimming pool near my house but I can swim in the sea.
I love sports.

Brazil

Phillippines

My name is Jasmine and I'm from Manila in the Phillippines. My favourite pastime is listening to music.
I like going to the music shop and buying CDs.
I sometimes go to concerts.
I also like surfing the Net. I chat with friends from all over the world.

Germany

Hi, I'm Wolfgang from Hamburg, Germany.
I love playing the guitar. But my favourite pastime is reading. I like reading adventure books and comics. It's like travelling. I go to the city library every week.
I also like going to the cinema with my friends.

Quiz. How many questions can you answer?

1. What does Raul do in his free time?
2. Is there a swimming pool near his house?
3. What's Jasmine's favourite pastime?
4. What does she do on the Net?
5. What does Wolfgang do in his free time?
6. What does Wolfgang do with his friends?

3 Free time

7 Sounds like fun

It's so c**oo**l eating f**oo**d by the p**oo**l.
He says, "It's g**oo**d, but I'm f**u**ll," and
opens his b**oo**k.

8 Language puzzle

Are there any salads?

No, there aren't.

Yes, there are.

Yes, there is.

Is there any pizza?

No, there isn't.

9 Write about your free time.

My favourite pastime is...

I usually...

I like watching ... on TV.

There's a/isn't any...

There are some/aren't any...

I sometimes/always go...

I also like...

10 Project: Make a poster about your favourite pastime.

MY FAVOURITE PASTIME

Stephenie Blair

My favourite pastime is playing the violin. This is a picture of me playing at the school concert.

I love listening to folk music. This is a photo of my favourite violin player. She's from England.

I also like going to the cinema with my friends at the weekend.

4 Holidas in the city

15 **1** Listen and sing the song.

Holidays in the City

We're going to the city,
We're going to have fun,
By boat or plane or bus or train,
Come and see it everyone.

People are friendly in the city.
We're going to see great sights.
The parks are bigger in the city,
And we're going to love the lights.

We're going to the city,
We're going to have fun,
By taxi, tram or underground,
Come and see it everyone.

They've got a stadium in the city,
And more interesting places to go.
They've got an aquarium in the city.
And you can see a fabulous show.

We're going to the city,
Where we're going to have fun,
By boat or plane or bus or train,
Come and see it everyone.
By taxi, tram or underground,
Come and see it everyone.
By car or on a motorbike,
Come and see it everyone.
Come and see it every one.

2 Ask a classmate about his perfect city.

Is there a zoo in your perfect city?

Yes, there's a zoo and an amusement park.

theatre – stadium
aquarium – museum – park
cinema – airport – port
underground – tram
train station – amusement
park

21 [twenty-one]

Holidays in the city

bicycle – motorbike – car
underground – taxi – bus
train – plane – boat

  17 **4** Listen and point. Then talk to a classmate.

opposite – next to
near – in – between
in front of – behind

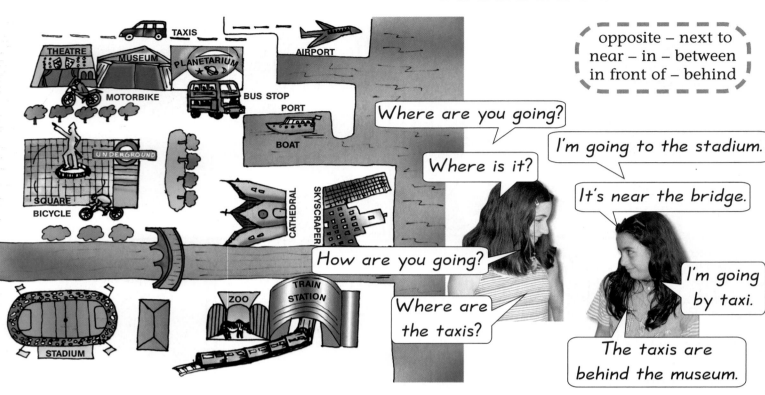

Where are you going?

Where is it?

I'm going to the stadium.

It's near the bridge.

How are you going?

Where are the taxis?

I'm going by taxi.

The taxis are behind the museum.

5 Compare the different types of transport.

Bicycles Buses Trains Taxis Planes	are	slower faster cheaper more expensive more comfortable more dangerous	than	bicycles. buses. trains. taxis. planes.

Taxis are faster than buses.

Yes, but buses are cheaper.

6 Speak about the different cities.

Seville   Quebec   Chicago   London

Seville is very hot.

Yes, Seville is hotter than Quebec.

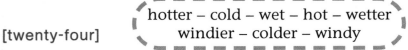
hotter – cold – wet – hot – wetter
windier – colder – windy

7 **Our world: My holiday**
Read and do the quiz.

Dublin, Ireland

Miami, Florida

My name is John Walsh and I'm from Dublin, Ireland. Dublin's wet most of the year. I'm going to Miami to visit some friends. The weather in Miami is hotter than in Dublin. The roads and cars are bigger. I think the people are more interesting. Everything is cheaper in Miami. It's going to be great fun.

My name is Jill Cohen and I'm from Miami, USA. Miami's got a tropical climate. I'm going on holiday to Dublin. I'm going to visit my Irish cousins. The weather in Ireland is colder than in Florida. It's sometimes windy and it rains a lot. I think Dublin is more expensive than Miami. The people are friendly but I think Miami is more beautiful.

Quiz: How many questions can you answer?

1. Has Miami got hotter weather than Dublin?
2. Has Miami got got smaller roads?
3. Has Dublin got a tropical climate?
4. Has Miami got bigger cars?
5. Has Dublin got friendly people?
6. Has Miami got more interesting people?
7. Has Dublin got colder weather?
8. Has Dublin got wetter weather.

4 Holidays in the city

18 **8** **Sounds like fun**

Down south by the sandy beaches, what
can you see
That's for splashing, swimming, sailing
And tastes like salt to me?

9 **Language puzzle**

| London | | colder | | | Seville. |

is

| Seville | | hotter | | than | London. |

| Trains | are | more comfortable | | | buses. |

10 **Write about two cities.
Compare them.**

I live in ... . My city is
bigger/smaller than ... .
The weather is hotter/colder
than ... . It's a
beautiful/attractive city.
I like/don't like ... because
it is more interesting/boring
than my city. In ... there
are more museums/cinemas/
... than in ... .

11 **Project: Make a tourist
brochure about your town.**

My town
Noel Brown

I sometimes
go fishing in
the river.

I live in a small town.
There is an interesting
castle in the centre of the
town.

There are
woods near
the town with
quiet paths.
I sometimes
play with my
friends in the
woods.

There is a beautiful river
flowing through the town.

My town
is famous
for race
horses.

1 Listen and say the poem.

The old castle

Dracula's castle was very old.
The large, dark rooms were very cold.
The castle door was strong and wide.
But something scary was there inside.

Dracula's picture was on the wall,
At the end of the long dark hall.
His eyes were red. His face was white.
His teeth were long and ready to bite.

The hall was long and full of spiders
And the bathrooms were full of lizards.
The cellar was dark and full of bats,
The bedrooms were full of toads and rats.

I was scared of the ghosts and rats,
The toads and bats, the spiders and cats.
And I was all alone that night,
In Dracula's castle in the pale moonlight.

 2 Ask a classmate.

Can you describe the castle?

The hall was full of spiders. The rooms were dark and cold.

Mike and Emma were with a group of tourists.

Count Dracula still walks these corridors.

I don't believe in ghosts.

Are you sure?

1

They were behind the group.

This is boring. Let's explore.

Follow me.

Are you sure?

2

They were in a long dark corridor.

I think this was a bad idea.

But you don't believe in ghosts.

3

What was that noise?

Maybe it was the wind.

4

They went upstairs to investigate the strange noise.

Let's go back.

Scaredy cat!

5

The noise was from inside the room.

Over there! In that room!

Maybe the guide is looking for us.

Come on chicken.

6

Dracula's picture was on the wall.

He was very handsome.

What about those teeth?

7

Long ago

4 Meet Dracula's family. Listen and match. Then ask a classmate.

Lucretia   Boris

Who's Dracula's daughter?

I think it's Rita.

son – daughter – grandfather
brother – sister – cousin – uncle
aunt – grandmother – father
mother

Dracula   Mortitia

Elvira   Igor

Frankie   Wolfi   Rita

Vampi

5 Listen and point. Then tell a classmate.

His sister was at the disco last night.

sister – grandfather and grandmother – uncle and aunt – father – mother

at the cinema – at home
at the restaurant – at the library
at the supermarket – at the disco

yesterday   last Saturday   last night

on Wednesday   on Monday   on Thursday

6 Ask a classmate.

Were	you	at the cinema	yesterday?	Yes, I was.
		at school	last Saturday?	No, I wasn't.
	they	at home	on Monday?	Yes, they were.
		in the park		No, they weren't.

Were you at home last Saturday?

Where were you?

No, I wasn't.

I was at the cinema.

7 **Our world: Buildings**
Read and do the quiz.

Castles

Castles were spectacular on the outside. But they weren't comfortable inside. The rooms were always dark because the windows were very small. The walls, floors and roof were very strong but very cold. A fireplace was the only way to heat the castle. The rooms were full of smoke. They were very uncomfortable.

Houses

The first houses were natural caves. Then people used wood, earth and stone. Ice was a building material in the frozen north. Modern houses now have gardens and garages. The windows are bigger and the furniture is better. Now houses are warmer, brighter and more comfortable.

The Sagrada Familia

Antonio Gaudi was born in Reus, Catalonia, Spain, in 1852. He wasn't very brilliant at school. But later he was a great architect and his buildings were very famous. He was a great innovator. The *Sagrada Familia* in Barcelona is his most famous building.

Quiz: **How many questions can you answer?**

1. Were medieval castles cold and dark?
2. Were the rooms comfortable?
3. Were the first houses natural caves?
4. Was ice a building material in the frozen north?
5. Was Antonio Gaudi a great singer?
6. Is the *Sagrada Familia* his most famous work?

5 Long ago

In the dark castle park there's a fat black cat, **a** bat and **a** rat.

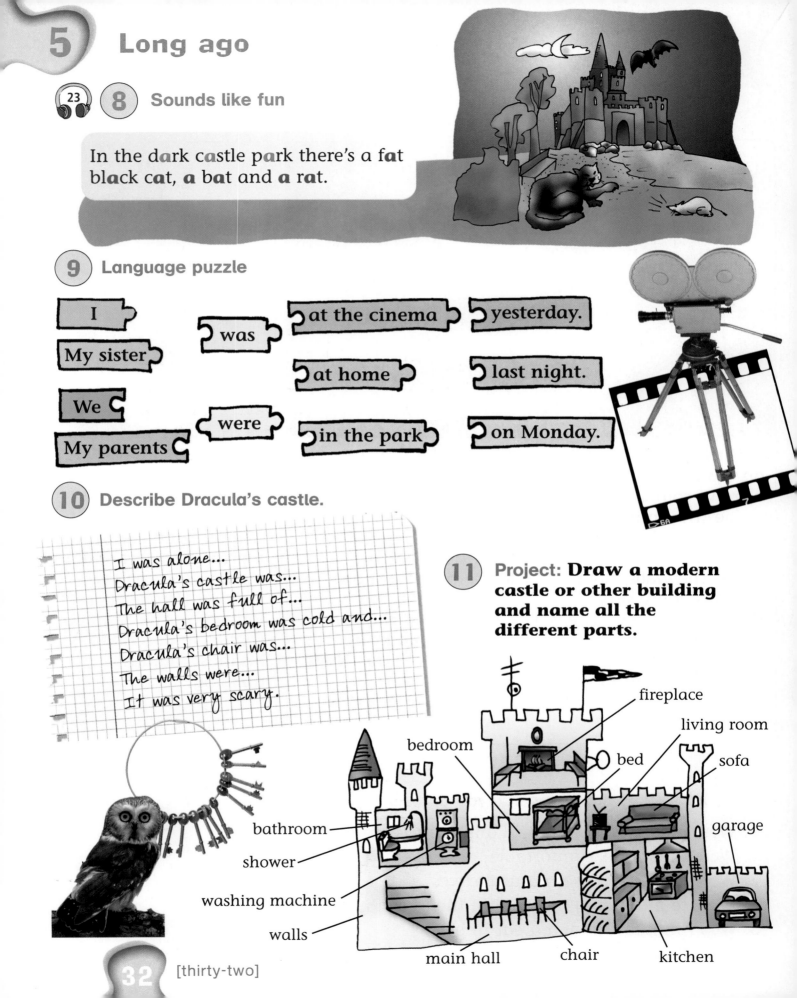

9 Language puzzle

I		at the cinema	yesterday.
My sister	was		
		at home	last night.
We	were		
My parents		in the park	on Monday.

10 Describe Dracula's castle.

I was alone...
Dracula's castle was...
The hall was full of...
Dracula's bedroom was cold and...
Dracula's chair was...
The walls were...
It was very scary.

11 Project: **Draw a modern castle or other building and name all the different parts.**

fireplace
living room
bedroom
bed
sofa
bathroom
garage
shower
washing machine
walls
main hall
chair
kitchen

6 Inventions

 1 Listen and sing the song.

The Good Old Days

Life was different in the good old days.
Now, life is better in so many ways.

There weren't any computers then.
There was only writing with paper and pen.
They used gas lamps to give them light.
They played in the streets till late at night.

Life was different in the good old days.
Now, life is better in so many ways.

Now we've got e-mail, and DVDs,
Television, microwaves and MP3s.
There are new inventions every day.
But is life better now in every way?

Life was different in the good old days.
Now, life is better in so many ways.

Now we've got video and mobile phones,
Internet and computer games
There wasn't any Internet then.
But people still had lots of fun.

Life was different in the good old days.
And just as good in many ways.

2 Talk to a classmate.

I think life was better in the old days.

Because children played in the street.

Why?

Why?

I think life is better now.

Because we've got computers.

Inventions

4 Listen, match and speak.

played – walked – cleaned
helped – prepared – talked
worked – lived

When I was young...

When Emma's great grandmother was young she played games with her friends.

5 Ask a classmate. 100 years ago.

Was there any e-mail one hundred years ago?

No, there wasn't.

Were there any cameras one hundred years ago?

Yes, there were.

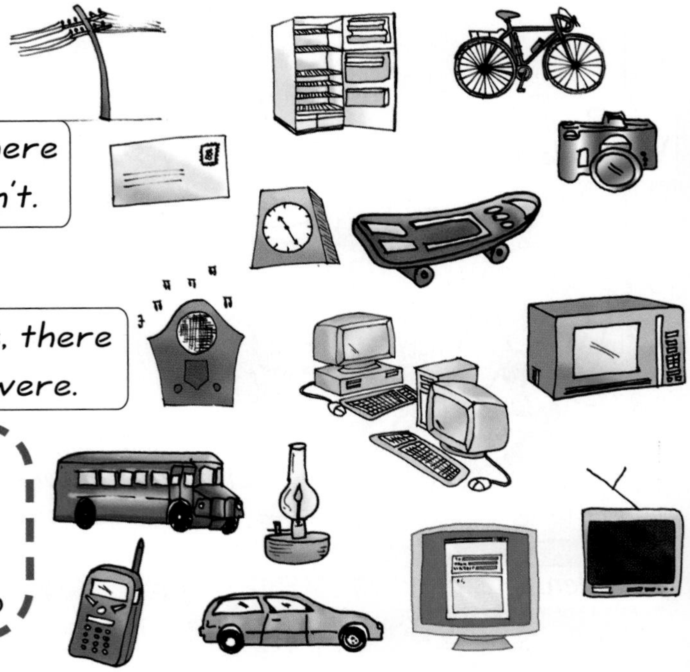

e-mail – cameras – computers
buses – clocks – bicycles
skateboard – microwave ovens
refrigerators – electricity
television – internet – post – radio

6 Talk to a classmate.

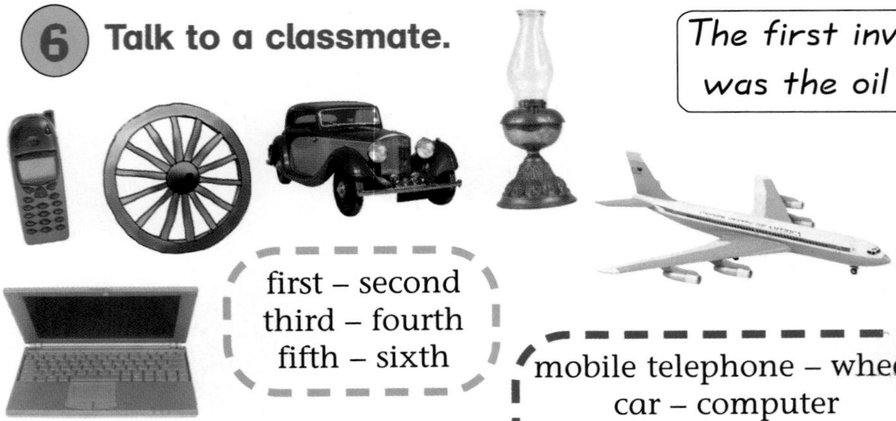

The first invention was the oil lamp.

first – second
third – fourth
fifth – sixth

mobile telephone – wheel
car – computer
oil lamp – plane

I don't agree. I think the wheel was the first invention.

7 **Our world: Inventions**
Read and do the quiz.

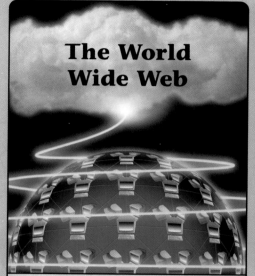

The World Wide Web

Jigsaw puzzles

PEA SOUP

CHOICE ▽ QUALITY

The tin can

In 1990 there wasn't a World Wide Web. Tim Berners-Lee invented the WWW in 1991. This connected millions of computers around the world. Before that, we always used libraries, walked to the newsagents, phoned the travel agent and went shopping. Now many people do all these things on the World Wide Web.

In 1766 there weren't any jigsaw puzzles. In 1767 John Spilsbury invented the jigsaw puzzle. He was a geography teacher. He wanted to help his students. He used a saw to cut out the countries and painted the pieces. This was the first jigsaw puzzle!

In 1809 there weren't any tin cans. Peter Durand invented the tin can in 1810. Large armies used a lot of food and the tin can preserved the food and saved many lives. Explorers needed the tin can to travel across deserts and up mountains. People then waited many years for a good can opener.

Quiz: True or False?

1. Tim Berners invented the WWW in 1919.
2. The WWW connected millions of computers.
3. John Spilbury invented the jigsaw puzzle in 1967.
4. He painted the countries with a saw.
5. Peter Durand invented the tin can in 1810.
6. The tin can helped explorers and armies.

6 Inventions

8 Sounds like fun

They plann**ed** and prepar**ed**.
They talk**ed** and work**ed**.
They invent**ed** and creat**ed**.

9 Language puzzle

was

wasn't any

electricity.

There

were

cars.

weren't any

Was

Were

there any

electricity?

cars?

10 Project: **Write about your invention.**
Draw it and name the parts.

MY SUPER-SKATEBOARD
This is my invention. It's a skateboard with a
motor. I can ride it to school. It is made of
wood, metal and plastic. All my friends want to
have the same wonderful skateboard.

stabilizer

body

fins

rocket motor

wheels

1 Listen and sing the song.

Robin Hood

Robin Hood, Robin Hood.
He lived long long ago.
Robin Hood, Robin Hood.
He always used a bow.

He was very strong.
He wore his hair quite long.
He fought the evil king.
But he still found time to sing.

Robin Hood, Robin Hood.
One thing we know for sure,
Robin Hood, Robin Hood.
He always helped the poor.

He lived in Sherwood forest
With all his merry men.
They practised with their swords
But they still found time to sing.

Robin Hood, Robin Hood.
He lived long long ago.
Robin Hood, Robin Hood.
Robin Hood, Robin Hood.

 2 Talk to a classmate.

Tell me about Robin.

He had long brown hair.

Robin and his father were hungry. They killed a deer in the forest.

Look, father! Soldiers.

Run, Robin, run!

1

Robin escaped from the soldiers, but without his father. Then he found some people in the forest.

What are you doing here?

We live in the woods.

We are hiding from the Sheriff of Nottingham and his soldiers.

2

Robin spoke to Maid Marion.

Your father's not dead. The Sheriff's men took him to Nottingham.

3

They had an idea.

I can help him. Please, show me the way to Nottingham.

All right, come with me.

4

They hid behind a bush.

Look, there's one of the Sheriff's soldiers.

Let's wait until he's very close.

5

Robin took the soldier's clothes.

Help!

I've got him!

6

Robin said goodbye to Marion.

Bye-bye, Robin. Take care and good luck. Come back again.

Yes, but only with my father.

7

Robin spoke to the guard.

Robin found his father.

Robin rode away.

Robin Hood

30 **4** Listen and match. Then describe and guess the people.

LITTLE JOHN   ROBIN HOOD   MAID MARION   THE SHERIFF

> He was tall and thin.
> He had long brown hair.
> He wore green clothes.
> He was brave and kind.

> That's Robin Hood.

Body: tall – short – fat – thin – strong – weak
Face: beautiful – handsome – ugly
Hair: long – short – straight – curly
Personality: kind – brave – bad – good – dangerous
Clothes: trousers – shirt – shoes – boots – hat – coat – skirt

5 Ask a classmate.

> Who was the tallest?

> Robin Hood was the tallest.

tallest – shortest – fattest
thinnest – strongest
weakest – most beautiful
most handsome – ugliest
youngest – oldest

31 **6** Listen and match. Then ask a classmate.

> How do you feel?

> I feel tired.

(a)   (b)   (c)   (d)   (e)

tired – sad – angry
worried – happy

7 Quiz: **Choose the correct answer. Then listen and check.**

1. Robin Hood lived around the year
   - a. 520.
   - b. 1180.
   - c. 1810.

2. Robin Hood lived
   - a. in a big town.
   - b. on a farm.
   - c. in a forest.

3. Robin Hood
   - a. gave money to the poor.
   - b. loved to sing for the king.
   - c. took money from the poor.

4. The Sheriff of Nottingham was
   - a. Robin's best friend.
   - b. Robin's father.
   - c. Robin's enemy.

 8 Our world: **Robin Hood**
Read and do the quiz.

In Robin's time many children never went to school. They worked in the fields and helped with the animals. The King, Richard the Lionheart, was often away from England. When he was away, life was very hard for the poor people. The rich took everything and sometimes hungry people hunted deer in the King's forest. When the Sheriff of Nottingham caught them, he killed them. He was the most dangerous man in Nottingham. But there were people in the forest who fought the Sheriff. They were Robin Hood and his friends. Robin was the bravest man in the forest.

Quiz. **True or False?**

1. At the time of Robin Hood children always went to school.
2. Richard the Lionheart was not always in England.
3. When the King was away the poor people were happy.
4. People were afraid of the Sheriff of Nottingham.
5. Some people in the forest fought the Sheriff.
6. Robin Hood lived in London.

7 Robin Hood

33 **9** Sounds like fun

The **v**illain was **v**ery **v**iolent, but Ro**b**in was the **b**est with the **b**ow.

10 Language puzzle

Robin Hood — took — money — from the rich.
— gave — — to the poor.

He — was — the **kindest** — and — **bravest.**
— the **most handsome.**

11 Describe a famous historical character.

Christopher Columbus

He was short and ... .
He had long ... hair and he was very ... .
He wore... .
He was brave and ... .

He was born in ... .
He's very famous because he ...
America in ... .
He died in ... .

12 Project: **Make a poster of the character.**

CHRISTOPHER COLUMBUS
COLUMBUS' DISCOVERY 1492 – 1493

Greenland

North America

Europe

Atlantic Ocean

Africa

South America

34 **1** Listen and sing the song.

Take Care

Listen, everybody to what I'm going to say,
Listen well and follow these rules, ok?
Hey, hey!

Take care when you are riding your bike.
Wear your helmet so that you're safe.
Take care when you're rollerblading.
Don't forget to put on your pads.

Take care when travelling in a car.
Remember to put on your safety belt!
Take care when you are crossing the street.
Remember to look to the right and left!

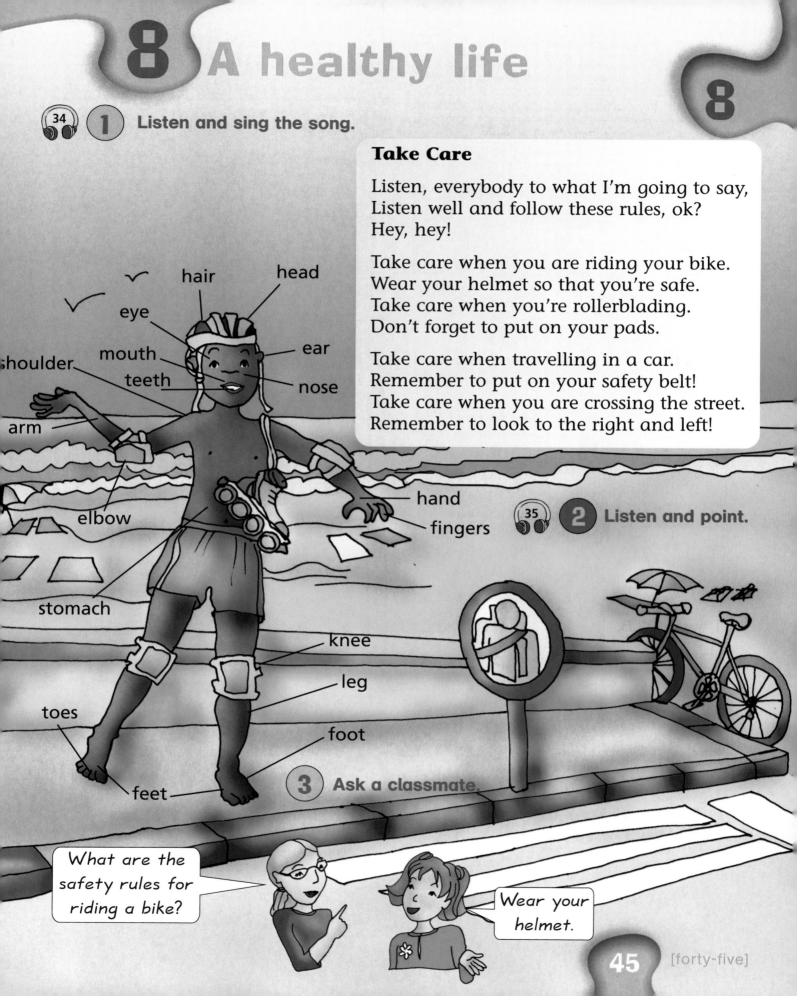

hair

head

eye

mouth

ear

shoulder

teeth

nose

arm

elbow

hand

fingers

35 **2** Listen and point.

stomach

knee

leg

toes

foot

feet

3 Ask a classmate.

What are the safety rules for riding a bike?

Wear your helmet.

A healthy life

  5 Listen to the stories and point.

	SITUATION 1	SITUATION 2
Question	• doctor • hospital • police	• doctor • hospital • police
Information	• in the park • opposite the park • behind the station	• in Green Street • next to the station • next to the police station
Problem	earache problem with his knee broken leg	earache problem with her arm broken knee
Help	• plaster • bandage • medicine	• plaster • bandage • medicine

6 Tell a classmate about the stories.

In situation 1 2	a man and his... a woman and her...		went to ...
The	doctor's house hospital	was	behind... next to... opposite...
The	boy girl	had	a problem with... a broken...
The doctor	put gave	a bandage round... ...in plaster. the boy the girl	some medicine.

Our world: A healthy body
Read and do the quiz.

Jane

Jane always eats healthy food and does exercise. She goes to bed early and sleeps for eight hours. Her favourite exercise is yoga. She does it every morning. She eats lots of fresh vegetables. She never eats junk food. Her friend Julie likes team sports. She plays volleyball with the school team.

Rachel

Hi, I'm Rachel. I'm a nutritionist. I help people to eat well. Some people are overweight. They need to control their diet. It's important to eat fresh food and drink enough water. A body needs vitamins and minerals. Vitamin C helps to prevent colds. Iron is good for the blood. Calcium is necessary for healthy bones. Get enough sleep.

Jimmy

Hello, my name is Jimmy. I'm a swimming coach. I help people to exercise well. You need to do some exercise every day. There are many different team and individual sports. There is a perfect sport for everybody. My team is training hard at the moment and exercising a lot. Next year we are going to the national finals.

Quiz. How many questions can you answer?

1. How much sleep do we need?
2. What does a body need to grow?
3. What minerals do we need?
4. Why do we need calcium?
5. Why do we need iron?

8 A healthy life

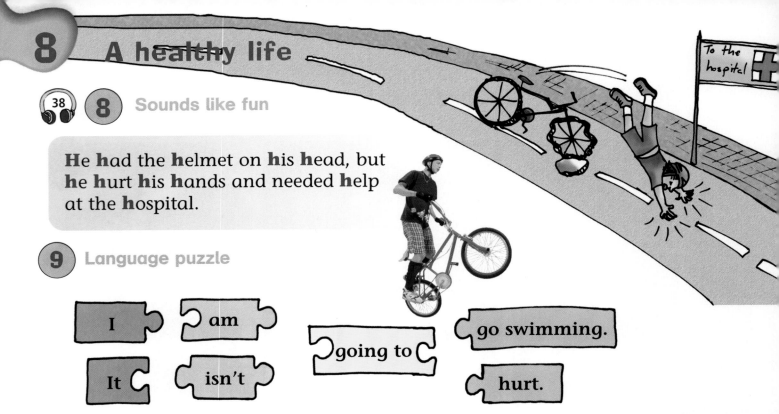

38 **8** Sounds like fun

He **h**ad the **h**elmet on **h**is **h**ead, but **h**e **h**urt **h**is **h**ands and needed **h**elp at the **h**ospital.

9 Language puzzle

I am

It isn't

going to

go swimming.

hurt.

10 Write about something that happened to you.

An accident

When I was ten...
I was on holiday in...
I hurt my...
I had a...
I went to...
The doctor gave me...
My parents...

11 Project: **Make a poster about junk food and healthy food.**

Make a list of each type of food.
What are you going to do to have a healthy life?

A HEALTHY LIFE

Eat ✓
fish
vegetables
fruit

Don't eat ✗
fast food
sweets
too many cakes

Exercise ✓
running
basketball
swimming

Don't ✗
watch too much tv
sit down for too long

Sleep ✓
8 hours

Don't ✗
stay up late

9 A Better World

  1 **Listen to the song.**

We're the children of this world

We're the children of this world.
We're the grown-ups of tomorrow.
Let's make the world a better place,
Without poverty and sorrow.

Why don't you stop the wars
And build more schools?
How can we learn
To live together?

We want to listen
To each other.
We want to live
In peace forever.

We're the children of this world.
We're the grown-ups of tomorrow.
Let's make the world a better place,
Without poverty and sorrow.

2 **Ask a classmate.**

How can we make the world a better place?

We can stop the wars.

1

2

3

4

5

6

A better world

4 Listen and match. Then ask a classmate.

Femi

Emma

Karen

Emma's aunt

Does Femi admire
Jane Goodall?

Why?

Yes, he does.

Because she's helping
chimpanzees in Africa..

Jane Goodall
Neil Amstrong
Nelson Mandela
Alexander Fleming

discovered penicillin
fights for black people's rights
is helping chimpanzees
went to the moon

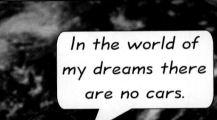

5 Talk to a classmate about the world
of your dreams.

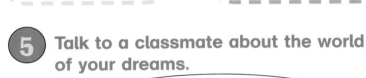
In the world of my dreams...

In the world of
my dreams there
are no cars.

...there are	not many no a lot of big friendly	mobile phones. computers. cars. gardens. people. plants.
...there are	more less bigger friendlier more beautiful better	bicycles. parks. people. streets. animals. sports centres. schools.
...children have got the	most beautiful friendliest longest best most interesting	schools. playgrounds. parents. friends. holidays. books.

In the world of
my dreams there
are bigger parks.

6 **Our world: Someone I admire**
Read and do the quiz.

Mahatma Gandhi

Gandhi was a pacifist. He studied law in London. He worked for human rights in India. He was in prison twice. His non-violence movement ended British rule in India. An assassin killed him in 1948.

He said: *Non-violence is the greatest force at the disposal of mankind.*

Aung San Suu Kyi

Aung San Suu Kyi fights for democracy in Burma. She was in prison. Her enemies tried to kill her but she survived. She received the Nobel Peace Prize in 1991 for her good work in Burma.

She said: *The only real prison is fear, and the only real freedom is freedom from fear.*

Marie Curie

Marie Curie was from Warsaw, Poland. She studied Physics and Mathematics in Paris. She discovered radium. She received the Nobel Prize in Chemistry in 1911. She died in France in 1934.

She said: *All my life through, the new sights of Nature made me rejoice like a child.*

Martin Luther King Jr.

Martin Luther King was from Georgia, in the USA. He fought for civil rights for Afro-Americans. He received the Nobel Peace Prize when he was thirty-five. An assassin killed him in 1968.

He said: *I have a dream that my four little children will one day live in a nation where they will not be judged by the colour of their skin, but by the content of their character.*

Quiz. How many questions can you answer?

1. Why was Martin Luther King an important person?
2. Why was San Suu Kyi in prison?
3. Who worked for human rights?
4. How many times was Gandhi in prison?
5. Where was Marie Curie from?
6. How old was Martin Luther King when he received the Nobel Peace Prize?

9 A better world

> **Cease** war! We want p**eace**!
> Said the people of Gr**eece**!

8 Language puzzle

I admire — her / him — because — he / she — fights for... / is helping... / was the inventor of... / discovered ....

9 Project: **Make a poster or write an article about someone you admire for the school newspaper.**

NEIL ARMSTRONG

The person I admire is Neil Armstrong.

He's a famous astronaut.

He was the first man to walk on the moon.

I think he's the greatest modern explorer.

I want to do something important for the world when I grow up.

CHILDHOOD

OHIO, 1930.

HE STUDIED AERONAUTICAL ENGINEERING.

HE WAS A NAVY PILOT.

"APOLLO 11"

IN 1969 HE WALKED ON THE MOON.

HE WAS A UNIVERSITY TEACHER.

HE IS NOW RETIRED AND LIVING ON A FARM IN OHIO.

Halloween

 43 Listen and sing the song.

Who's there?

Who's that?

It's us.

It's us. The witches, monsters and ghosts.

 Read the text and answer the questions.

Halloween

On 31st October, children in Britain, Ireland and the USA dress up as witches, monsters and ghosts. They go from house to house and ring the doorbell. When the door opens they shout, "trick or treat". People give the children a treat: sweets, nuts or fruit. Some people don't give anything. Then the children play a trick. They ring the doorbell again and run away. There are also Halloween parties. A favourite game is snap apple. First hang an apple by the stem with a string. Then try to bite the apple with your teeth. Do not use your hands.

Halloween Song

Give us a treat, (oh, yeah),
Give us a treat, (oh, yeah),
Give us a treat or
We'll play a trick on you!

It's trick or treat, (oh, yeah),
It's trick or treat, (oh, yeah),
It's trick or treat, or
We'll get you, too!

It's the last night of October,
We knock on every door,
But sometimes people lock us out
And then they can hear us shout:

Give us a treat, (oh, yeah),
Give us a treat, (oh, yeah),
Give us a treat or
We'll play a trick on you!

It's trick or treat, (oh, yeah),
It's trick or treat, (oh, yeah),
It's trick or treat, or
We'll get you, too!

1. When is Halloween?

2. What do the children do on Halloween night?

3. What games do they play?

Thanksgiving

1 The story about Thanksgiving

It is 1620. The Mayflower lands in America. The ship comes from England.
The people on the Mayflower are looking for a new home. It is winter.
The people from England are cold and hungry. Native Americans help
them to build houses. They show them how to hunt for wild turkey. They
show them how to catch fish. Later, when it is warm again,
they show them how to plant corn. The people want to
thank the Native Americans and have a big party. They invite
the Native Americans. They call their party Thanksgiving.

Answer the questions.

1. Why is the Mayflower in America?
2. Who helped them to build their houses?
3. What do the Native Americans show them?
4. Why do they call the party Thanksgiving?

2 Thanksgiving day

The fourth Thursday of November is a holiday in the United States.
It's Thanksgiving. On this day, all the family come together and have a big dinner.
People usually eat turkey, sweet potatoes and other vegetables. They have pumpkin
pie for dessert. There are also big parades in the streets. Everybody has lots of fun.

Answer the questions.

1. When is Thanksgiving?
2. Where is it celebrated?
3. What do people do on this day?
4. What do people usually eat
   on Thanksgiving?

World Book Day

1 **What's World Book Day?**

World Book Day is a special day to celebrate books and reading. More than thirty countries celebrate World Book Day. The festival first started in Catalonia, Spain. The people gave presents of roses and books on St. George's Day, or San Jordi. This tradition started in 1926 in memory of Miguel de Cervantes.

World Book Day in the UK and Ireland is celebrated in March or April. There are many special events to celebrate the day. Children receive a World Book Day book token to buy a book. The idea is to help children to explore the pleasure and enjoyment of reading.

Read the text and answer the questions.

1. When is World Book Day?
2. Where did the festival begin?
3. When is World Book Day celebrated in the UK and Ireland?
4. What do the children get on that day?

2 **Write about your favourite book then talk about it in class.**

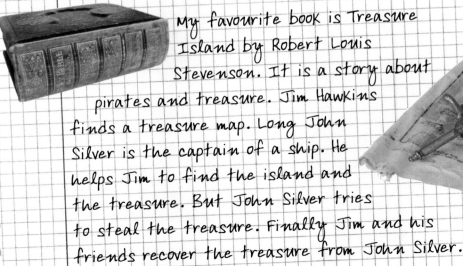

My favourite book is Treasure Island by Robert Louis Stevenson. It is a story about pirates and treasure. Jim Hawkins finds a treasure map. Long John Silver is the captain of a ship. He helps Jim to find the island and the treasure. But John Silver tries to steal the treasure. Finally Jim and his friends recover the treasure from John Silver.

Revision game

1. When's your birthday?
2. What are your hobbies?
3. What's your favourite school subject?
4. Name three classroom objects.

16. Name three types of transport.
15. Name three places to go in the city.
14. Where are you going on holiday?
13. What can we have for lunch?

17. Is Seville hotter than Quebec?
18. Has Ireland got smaller roads than Florida?
19. Can you describe the castle?
20. Name three rooms.

32. What are the safety rules when crossing the street?
31. Name six body parts.
30. People were afraid of the Sheriff of Nottingham. True/False
29. Robin took from the poor and gave to the rich. True/Fa...

33. What's the matter?
34. How many stitches has Femi got?
35. How much sleep do we need?
36. What does a body need to grow?

⑤ What's this?

What are you doing to save the planet? ⑥

⑦ It lives in a hole. It eats fish. It's a bird.

Does it eat grass? ⑧

⑫ What's in the fridge?

Name three places to go in your free time. ⑪

What can you do in your town? ⑩

Name three animals in danger of extinction. ⑨

Where were Mike and Emma on holiday? ㉑

Who's Dracula's daughter? ㉒

Were you at the cinema yesterday? ㉓

㉔ What was the first invention?

Describe Robin Hood. ㉘

The tin can helped explorers and armies. True/False. ㉗

Name three inventions. ㉖

㉕ When was the WWW invented?

How can we make the world a better place? ㊲

㊳ Why was Gandhi an important person?

Who do you admire a lot? ㊴

In the world of your dreams there are... ㊵

Language reference

Unit 1

What's your name?

What's your favourite school subject?

Where are you from?

Where do you live?

When's your birthday?

Who's that boy?

How old are you?

Do you like London?	Yes, I **do.**
	No, I **don't.**
Are you from London?	Yes, I **am.**
	No, I'**m not.**
Is London the capital of England?	Yes, it **is.**
	No, it **isn't.**

Unit 2

Is it small?	Yes, it **is.**
Has it **got** feathers?	Yes, it **has.**
Does it eat grass?	No, it **doesn't.**

What'**s** the tiger do**ing**?   It'**s** hunt**ing.**

Unit 3

There **is some** juice.
There **are some** crisps.

Is there **any** juice?	Yes, there is.
Are there **any** crisps?	No, there aren't.

Unit 4

London is cold**er** than Seville.

Seville is hott**er** than London.

Trains are **more** comfortable **than** buses.

Unit 5

I / He /She	**was**	at the cinema	yesterday.		
		at home	last night.		
Was	he	in the park	yesterday?	Yes, he **was.**
	she	at work	on Monday?	No, she **wasn't.**

Units

Unit 6

There	was / wasn't any	electricity.
	were / weren't any	cars.
Was / Were	there any	electricity? / cars?

| I/You He/She/It We/They | phoned worked | yesterday. last week. on Tuesday. |

Unit 7

Robin **took** money from the rich.
He **gave** it to the poor.
Robin **found** his father.

He was the kind**est** and brav**est**.
He was the **most** handsome.

Unit 8

| I am not / It is/isn't | **going to** | eat junk food. / hurt. |

Unit 9

I admire him/her because he/she fights for peace.

Comparative/Superlative

cold	colder	coldest
cool	cooler	coolest
hot	hotter	hottest
small	smaller	smallest
big	bigger	biggest
fast	faster	fastest
slow	slower	slowest
cheap	cheaper	cheapest
friendly	friendlier	friendliest
interesting	more interesting	most interesting
beautiful	more beautiful	most beautiful
useful	more useful	most useful
good	better	best
bad	worse	worst

Irregular verb list

be	was/were
break	broke
cut	cut
fight	fought
find	found
give	gave
go	went
have	had
hurt	hurt
make	made
put	put
say	said
see	saw
speak	spoke
take	took
wear	wore

PUBLISHED BY THE PRESS SYNDICATE OF THE UNIVERSITY OF CAMBRIDGE
The Pitt Building, Trumpington Street, Cambridge, United Kingdom

CAMBRIDGE UNIVERSITY PRESS
The Edinburgh Building, Cambridge CB2 2RU, UK
40 West 20th Street, New York, NY 10011–4211, USA
477 Williamstown Rd, Port Melbourne, VIC 3207, Australia
Ruiz de Alarcón 13, 28014 Madrid, Spain
Dock House, The Waterfront, Cape Town, 8001, South Africa

IN ASSOCIATION WITH

ELI
P.O. Box 6 - 62019 Recanati - Italy

© Cambridge University Press and ELI, 2005

First published 2004

Printed and bound in Colombia by Imprelibros S.A.

Acknowledgements

Book design and layout by Beatriz Nieto Casado; José Luis G. Belderrain;
José Manuel Alonso and Raimundo Fernández Durán.
Cover design by Conectia, S.L.
Cover illustration by Delia Llana Fúnez.
Recorded material produced by Craig Stevenson (Brave Arts, S.L.).

The authors would like to thank the following individuals for their editorial work on
the course: José Luis García Belderrain, Anna Giménez González, Claudia Díaz
Piquero, Carmen Fernández Ruiz and Ane Ortiz from Cambridge University Press;
Enda O'Callaghan and Denyse M. Wang. The authors would also like to thank all
Cambridge sales staff in Spain for their feedback on the material and its suitability
for their teachers.

The authors and publishers would like to thank the following individuals and
institutions for their help in commenting on the original material and for the
invaluable feedback which they provided:
Alicia Abril Blanco (CP Francisco de Quevedo, Fuenlabrada), Javier Alfaya Hurtado
(CPR Fuenlabrada), Maripi Arriaga Aznar (CEIP Bernat de Riudemeia, Argentona),
María Becerra Pérez (CP Jorge Juan, Novelda), Sònia Bonjorn and Vega Fatjó (Sagrat
Cor Casp, Barcelona), Gaspar Bonmatí Abellán (CP L'Albacar, Benimarfull),
Montserrat Bosch (Escola TAU, Barcelona), Pilar Botella López (CP La Serranica,
Aspe), Amparo Cabrera (CP El Prado, Olivares), María Teresa Díaz López, Iziar
González-Andrio Giménez, Pilar Varela López and Isabel Villamor Pérez (CP
Aldebarán, Tres Cantos), Lourdes Lafuente (CP Cervantes, Fuenlabrada), Carmen
Martín Morgado (CP Fray Bartolomé de las Casas, Sevilla), Rosa Martínez (CP
Alfonso de Orleans, Utrera), Manuel Montes (Colegio Altair, Sevilla), Berta Nieto (CP
Julio Verne, Fuenlabrada), Noreen O'Donnell and Leticia Penzo (Col·legi Sant Ignasi,
Barcelona), Mercedes de la Ossa del Pozo (CP Antonio Machado, Elda), Ioia Panella
Balcells (CEP Santa Eulàlia, Sant Pere de Ribes), Raquel Royo (IES Francisco Figueras
Pacheco, Alicante), Blanca Esther Sánchez (CP Clara Campoamor, Fuenlabrada), Susi
Tello (CEIP Pilarín Bayés, Sant Quirze del Vallés), Emma Thomson (CLIC, Sevilla),
Manuel Toledo (Colegio Corpus Christi, Sevilla), Nicole Varano (Centro
Norteamericano de Estudios Interculturales, Sevilla).

Illustration and colour: Delia Llana Fúnez, Inmaculada Fernández Latorre,
Emma Ferguson and Conectia, S.L.

The publisher gratefully acknowledges the following for providing photographs:
Christine Genoud: Units 1 and 5.
Corbis: Faces of the World, Units 1 and 3; Film, Music, Dance, Units 1 and 3, Modern
Teen, Unit 4; Visions of Nature, Units 4 and 7.
Digital Stock: Animals and Wildlife, Unit 2; Children at Play, Unit 4; Destination
Europe, Unit 4; Destination Tropics, Unit 4; Digital Concepts, Unit 6; Retro Home &
Family, Unit 9.
Digital Vision: Unit 9.
Image DJ: Hands, Unit 9; Medical Supplies, Unit 8; Picture Potluck, Unit 6;
Texture, Unit 3.
Imgram Publishing: Imagelibrary 500 and 1000, Units 2, 3, 4, 5, 6, 7, 8,9 and Extra
units.
José Luis García Belderrain: Units 1, 2, 3, 4, 5, 6, 7 and 9.
Photodisc: Backgrounds and Objects, Units 7, 8 and Extra unit; Beauty and Health,
Unit 8; Everyday Animals, Units 2, 4 and 5; Infomedia 3, Unit 8; World Landmarks
and Travel, Unit 1.
Stockbyte: Contemporary lifestyles, Unit 1; Healthcare, Science & Discovery, Unit 8
and 9; Sport. The Will to Win, Unit 8

The Publisher would like to thank Colegio Ágora (Madrid), for all the help with the
photographs included in this course.

Every effort has been made to trace all the copyright holders but if any have been
inadvertently overlooked, the publishers will be pleased to make the necessary
arrangement at the first opportunity.